Bodies, Memories
And Spirits

*"For the memory of Harold Simmons . . .
and for the life and spirit of the Folk Research Centre."*

Bodies, Memories And Spirits

A Discourse On Selected Cultural
Forms And Practices Of St.lucia

Travis Weekes

To order additional copies of this book, contact:
Xlibris LLC
1-888-795-4274
www.Xlibris.com
Orders@Xlibris.com
552029

CONTENTS

INTRODUCTION

This book provides information on several of the key cultural forms and practices on the island of Saint Lucia. The author came to be interested in these phenomena through his work both as a theatre artist and as an educator on the island. Several of the Saint Lucia's dramatists particularly Nobel Laureate Derek Walcott and his twin brother Roderick, deceased, as well as the author, utilize Saint Lucia's cultural forms and practices in their plays. While employed with the Folk Research Centre as the Cultural Education Officer between the years 1997-1999, the author spent many hours within the walls of its small but valuable library foraging through the wealth of material available. Subsequently his research as a graduate student of Cultural Studies at the UWI, Cave Hill, sent him studying the Creole discourse in Saint Lucian culture and how this impacted the development of Saint Lucian theatre. It is the latter focus that influenced the selection of cultural forms and practices discussed in this book. Therefore while the work here would be of tremendous value to those who have a general interest in Saint Lucian Culture, they would also hold special value to students of Saint Lucian/Caribbean/Postcolonial Theatre.

THE KOUDMEN

Traditional work related activities associated with farming, fishing and house construction among the colonized were closely connected to survival and the provision of their basic needs. The *Koudmen* (Coup de Main) refers to an activity that engenders co-operative labour towards the execution of a particular project. The principle of the *Koudmen* is that of freely offering one's services to helping one's fellow man; a commitment to sharing his burden. The sharing of food, drink and music is an important input to lighten the burden while fostering a harmonization of efforts and energies. Underlying the principle of the Koudmen appears to be is a worldview that stresses the responsibility of the particular to the wider, the responsibility of the smaller household units to the extended family and of connected families to the broader community.

The principle of lightening the burden of one's fellow man structures the organization of the work related practices. Traditionally, practices tied to the work of the folk are facilitated by singing, drumming, storytelling and dancing. Brathwaite throws some light on how the performing arts came to be so closely related to work activities among the descendants of Africa in the Caribbean.

> "*Music and dance though recreational, were functional as well. Slaves, as in Africa, danced and sang at work, at play, at worship, from fear, from sorrow, from joy. Here was the characteristic form of their social and artistic expression.*[1]"

Some of those work practices of the descendants of Africans which revolved around woodcutting, farming and fishing actually developed into other cultural forms which came to be known as: The *Siyé Bwa, The Pichay*, and the *Gwajé Manyok*. The collective hauling of canoes into the sea on mornings to go fishing and pulling them back on shore on evenings is also fired by the spirit of the *Koudmen.*

Mintz and Price's theory that "the slaves needed to create new institutions to serve their everyday purposes" is a useful one for my analysis of work related cultural practices[2]. The definition by these authors of an institution as "any regular or orderly social interaction that acquires a normative character, and can hence be employed to meet recurrent needs" can be used quite aptly as a description of the Koudmen[3]. The story of Althius Tisson who resides at La Riviere Mitan, Monchy, provides invaluable insight into the tradition of the Siyé Bwa.

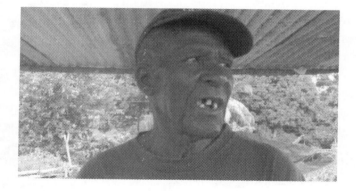

Althius Tisson was born in Dichlen a part of Monchy in the old district of Dauphin. His father was from Monier and his mother from Labonne, both communities also part of old Dauphin. Arthur began to learn the art of wood sawing as soon as he entered his teens. He learned from his father Emmanuel Tisson who had learned from his father before him. It was the family's legacy. Althius accompanied his father to work in several areas of the community such as the old parish of Dauphin, Foyal, Garrand, Balata, anywhere in the vicinity that was heavily forested. Althius speaks quite proudly of his profession: the art and craft runs in his blood he says and he describes his skill and mastery of the various stages involved in wood sawing:

Mwen ka siyé . . . na fè zézant . . . na koupé bwa–a . . . mwen ka fè tout kalté bagay épi an bwa mwen ka fè sa . . . mwen ka siyé menm . . . menm . . . menm . . . mwen ka koupé bwa–a, na hété'y atè–a . . . lè mwen fini mwen ka tonsé'y na bat li anlè . . . èk mwen ka kawé'y . . . mwen kawé'y . . . na fè chanté'y–a . . . lè mwen fini fè chanté'y–a . . . mwen vwéhé bwa–a mouté anlè . . . na chensé'y . . . bat li anlè'y . . . fè tout bagay èk lè mwen fini na èspéhé kamawad mwen vini pou nou mété siyan bwa–a.

In the early stages, Althius learned to saw the *Lòwyé (Laurier) Zabòka* . . . a tree that grows long leaves which can still be found on the *Barre de Lisle*. He also learned to saw the *Pòwyé* and other white wood that were used to produced planks of wood needed by the community.

However Althius and his family did not saw the *Gomier*, the tree from which the fishermen of old dug out their fishing canoe; one which Althius describes as being *méchan* (wicked). Yet he was well aware of the process of digging out the Gomier, having witnessed the practice near La Souciere, on Crown Lands, in the community of Chassin, Babonneau.

After the Gomier tree is cut and felled, one dug out the bottom of the canoe from within the trunk . . . then one sawed planks from the Laurier Canelles (a wood that can resist water) which one then fitted at the sides of the canoe for sufficient height. The canoe would then be placed on a *kabouwé* (cart) and hauled to the sea.

In the olden days, *Siyé Bwa* was an exciting cultural form. Family and friends across generations participated in the activity. There was plenty of music from the *Tanmbou* and *Ti bwa*. The women came and cooked food for the men. It was a huge Koudmen. What also made it exciting was that it took the form of a competition. There could be three sets of *Chantey* at any one time. The set that produced the most planks emerged as the winner. A bottle of rum would be placed where everyone could see it and the winner would get the prize. Yet afterwards the winning group shared the rum among all the competitors. That's how timber was produced in the olden days.

WORKSONG

Let us examine a work song from the *Siyé* recorded during a research activity organized by Simmons and Lomax in the year 1962. The participants are obviously aware of the objective of the session but are "Koudmen practitioners". Before the actual performance of the song, the speaker engages in a dramatic exposition of the principle underlying the Koudmen as it would apply to the task of log hauling. The singer is also interviewed after the performance. I have transcribed the session into St. Lucian Kwéyòl and translated the same into English.

Manmay la jòdi sanmedi
Annou mouté an bwa èk mwen
Sa ki ni bonn volonté
Pou nou alé, wédi an konnot épi mwen
Mwen ni donmbwé
Mwen ni donmbwé
Mwen ni vyann salé
Mwen ni fawin ek lanmowi, dité èk pen
(Na manje anpil wi gason)
Si ou ka manjé anpil, mwen ni pou mwen kontanté'w, dépi ou
ni bonn volanté.
(Ou ni wom-an?)
An sé mwen ki ni wom
La ni wom tèlman ou paka vlé kopwann
Manman sé tjè
Manmay-la mawé kannòt la byen eh
Nou wivé
Ou finn mawé?

Wè si i ni kòd pa dèyè'y
Si an kay ni pou balanché
(Wouzé gòj-mwen avan mwen pati)
Ou vle an wouzé
Alright mwen ka ba wou'y, pwen'y!

Folks, today is Saturday
Let us go to the forest with me.
All those who feel the spirit of sharing
Let's go haul down a canoe with me
I have dumpling
I have dumpling
I have salted beef
I have farine and saltfish, bread and tea,
(I eat plenty you k now boy)
If you eat plenty I have to satisfy you, once you feel the spirit of
help
(you have rum)
Is me that have rum
There is so much rum you won't want to understand

Manman is heart
Folks do tie the canoe securely
We have arrived
You've finished tying it?
See if there is rope behind it.
We would need to balance it.
(sprinkle my throat before we leave)
You want a sprinkled throat?
Alright I will sprinkle your throat. Take it.

It is important to note that this work is done solely through selfless cooperative effort, and all that needs to be provided is food and drink. This is the principle of the Koudmen. The speaker asks help from those who have "*bonne volonté* ", those who have the spirit of lending a helping hand to his fellow man, his brother. This is a value that is respected and again emphasized in the actual work-song which follows:

Ah tout wo!
Ay fwè-mwen
Ah tout wo!
Ay fwè mwen
A tout fwè-mwen na
Ay fwè-mwen
Tiwé mwen dan la twaka
Ay fwè-mwen
Tiwé mwen dan la mizè
Ay fwè-mwen
Mété mwen ay bòd lanmè
Ay fwè-mwen
Tiwé woy
Ay fwè-mwen
Tiwé . . . dan labawa
Ay fwè mwen
Tiwé . . . dan la twaka
Ay fwè mwen
Mwen vlé mwen ay bòd lanmè
Ay fwè—mwen
Tjebé kòd-la ban-mwen

Oh people!
Ay my brother
Oh people!
Ay my brother
Oh my brothers
Yes my brother
Take me out of trouble
Ay my brother
Take me out of misery
Ay my brother
Put me on the coast
Ay my brother
Take me out of . . .
Ay my brother
Take me out of difficulty
Ay my brother
Take me out of trouble

Ay my brother
Want to reach me down the coast
Ay my brother
Hold the rope for me.
Ay my brother

The singer sounds out a call to all and he receives a response from those who refer to him as their brother. The men move with the rhythm of the song and while they do so the singer guides, inspires and motivates them. It is no easy task hauling the canoe unto a cart and down to the coast. No one man can get it done all by himself. It is interesting that although their response is collective and in unison each one of them responds to him with the words my brother. It really means that they become one voice, one spirit, one effort and one rhythm. This is channeled into the form of the movement, and their bodies are energized into one. This is balanced by the absolute humility on his part as he asks them to help him out of trouble, out of difficulty, out of misery. His task is to haul a canoe that has been constructed some eight to ten miles up in the forest which he has to take down to the coast but he asks for help out of trouble, struggle, misery; appealing for assistance out of an underlying human condition which we can all feel, which we can all identify with. It is this common identity that makes his task, also that of his fellow man. They are all labourers together. Each man feels his brother's pain. This must be what Gilroy means when he says that "we need to consider, for example, how the emotional and affective bonds that form the specific basis of raciological and ethnic sameness are composed, and how they become patterned social activities with elaborate cultural features"[4].

THE PITJAY AND THE GWAJÉ MANIOC (MANYÒK)

The *Pitjay* refers to that cultural form used by the people of Labonne to plant manioc upon the Dauphin lands for the subsequent making of farine and cassava. While the Pitjay referred to the activity of planting the Manioc, the *Gwajé Manyok* referred to the grating of the manioc into farine to make cassava. The *Pitjay* involved working large areas of land and because of this several people were required. It was another variation of the Koudmen and participants gave of their time voluntarily.

During the *Pitjay* rows of men with pickaxes move (dance) in time to the rhythm of the drum as they dig holes into the ground. Rows of women move behind them with bags of manioc sticks which they place in the holes that have been dug. There are also other persons aiding the process, for example, a woman would pass between the labourers giving out rum and water without disturbing the rhythm of the digging and planting. There also others cooking a huge pot of food. Songs, following the typical call and response structure are sung by the workers, no doubt to inspire themselves but also to assist the function of keeping the time of their planting movements.

The *Gwajé Manyok* involved many people in the community working together throughout the night to grate large amounts of manioc because if they remained beyond the night they would spoil. The *Gwajé Manyok* is an activity that involves members of an extended family and/or community working together throughout an entire night to grate large amounts of manioc because if the roots were left beyond the night they would spoil. Bags of manioc sticks are grated on huge homemade graters into a large box for the preparation of farine and cassava the following day. Another version of the *Koudmen*, this otherwise mundane activity is also driven by drums, songs and the supply of food and drink by the host family.

St. Lucian Derek Walcott won the Nobel Prize for Literature in 1992, draws deeply upon St. Lucia's cultural forms and practices in his poetry and drama. Upon receiving the Nobel Prize Walcott attempted to use the spirit of the Koudmen to inspire support for a project that he had conceived entitled, The Rat Island Foundation.

Rat Island is a tiny island off the north of St. Lucia and Walcott's dream was to have established on that island a foundation that would organize writers' workshops that would facilitate exchange among local, regional and international writers. At the launch of the concept, Walcott delivered a speech in which he asserted:

It is not out duty to give any more than it is our duty to receive, but once we lose the tribal duty of help, the coup de main, we lose spirit, then a country. As we have lost the flight of pelicans.[5]

The Koudmen is still practiced in many of the rural communities of St. Lucia. Thus we have not lost "the tribal duty of help". However the challenge is to keep this spirit of the Koudmen alive and to cultivate it within other areas of the general community.

KOUTUMBA

The Koutumba was a dance ceremony held during the months of November and December. The Koutumba would also be held at any time of the year to mark the death of someone in the community. The ceremony would be held nine nights after the death of a family member. In writing of the Yoruba, Warner Lewis observes that ceremonies for the dead were of vital importance to all groups, particular attention being focused on the ninth night after death. Mintz and Price in writing of the continuity of African religions in Trinidad refer to the "kututo ceremony for the dead, which is held in November, and is now linked to a catholic mass for the souls in purgatory"[6]. The ritual of the *Koutumba* was marked by much drumming and the singing of many songs of loss, of farewell, but also of a celebration of the spirit world. Ethnographic research conducted by Harold Simmons and subsequently by the Folk Research Centre in St. Lucia, provides evidence that much of the drumming and dancing practices associated with the *Koutumba* are still practiced among a group of persons from Piaye, a community in the south of the island whose inhabitants consider themselves to be descendants of the Djiné.

Doudou as he is popularly known is the grandchild of one of the nineteenth century African immigrants on the island. In his prime, he was an unofficial cultural ambassador of Saint Lucia, spreading love and appreciation of the Koutoumba all around the island and beyond. The Piaye Dancers made up of younger persons of the community has inherited Doudou's legacy and continues to perform the dances of the Koutumba at various festivals in St. Lucia and in other parts of the Caribbean.

At the time of writing, Doudou was ninety two years old but still had vivid memories of the practice of the Koutumba when he was a child. His father was a drummer and a dancer of the Koutumba. Back then, the adults made tents out of wood and other natural resources from the environment such as coconut branches. Then at sundown they would gather under these tents to sing and dance. The boy Clifton would stick close to them observing and listening carefully to the songs. Often he would also join in the dances and the adults would marvel at his ability. His interest and enthusiasm paid off, for when the adults travelled to perform in different communities around the island, they would take Clifton along with them.

The dances of the Koutumba were guaranteed to be exchanged among communities. A bouquet of flowers was used as an interesting device to aid in galvanizing that process. The host community of the Koutumba would create a bouquet of flowers which they would hand to representatives of a visiting community. It would then be the responsibility of the recipients of the bouquet to hold the next Koutumba.

As an adult, Doudou's talent and childhood enthusiasm for the dances became an inspiration for many persons in his community and throughout St. Lucia. The Piaye Dancers, of which he was the respected 'star dancer" even into his eighties, became a feature at many cultural activities on the island and was often selected by the Folk Research Centre and the Cultural Development Foundation to represent the island at festivals overseas.

Yang mikiyang mikiyang kikango/ abélésé dé (repeat)

THE KONT

Kont is a popular community art form that is evidently an offshoot from the Koutumba. The songs of the *Kont* often narrate some aspect of the life of a deceased family member. Although common themes are sickness and death, the mood is often celebratory and this mood is enhanced by the vigourous drumming and dancing which follows the narrative of the song.

Kont through its French etymology "Conte" means "to tell, to relate". Thus in French Creole (Kweyol), *Kont* currently used, immediately connotes a particular form of singing, of dancing, of drumming. *Kont* also refers to the traditional storytelling form that took place eight nights after the passing of the loved one. As a participatory art form which utilizes drummers, singers, dancers, and storytellers, the *Kont* is a form has evolved in such a way, that members of the audience themselves are participants. Indeed there is hardly any distinction between audience and performers.

Traditionally, another variation of the *Kont* coincides (although in isolation) during the month of November with the Roman Catholic observance of All Souls Day. Traditionally, *Kont* runs as follows: the storyteller throws out a melody till he gets a response from the group. When the chorus does respond he intensifies the melody till he receives support from the drummers. As the rhythm increases he begins to dance, other dancers begin to interact until the storyteller takes control again and begins the story. Throughout the story the audience remains as full participants taking their cue from the storyteller as they continue to respond intermittently to his call, in song and chants. When he has finished his *listwa* (l'histoire) the space becomes completely overrun by the drumming, singing and dancing.

Fortunately, the research carried out in St. Lucia in the 1960's by Lomax and Simmons[7] point to definition of the *Kont* that is more reflective of its ontological significance to the people of African ancestry on the island than what the French name of the form confers. During this project Simmons conducted an interview with the descendants of the nineteenth century African immigrants in St. Lucia, one of whom was a chantwèl/chanteur who identified himself as Victor. The term chantwèl refers to the one who plays role of lead singer, but a chantwèl would also be a *kontè* (conteur) derived from French term 'raconteur' meaning the one who tells the story. The problem with these French terms is that neither of them encapsulates the complete function of one such as Victor, who takes the lead in the *Kont*.

The interview with Victor which was done in Kwéyòl, sheds light not only on the spiritual significance of the *Kont*, but also on the role of the *Kont* in the creolization process. The *Kont* was part of the ritual of African form of the 'wake', a ceremony held for the passing of a loved one, a custom which came over with the imported Africans. Victor explains that his people would hold a *Koutumba* regularly but particularly when an African dies. Victor is careful to make the distinction between the last surviving Africans who came after emancipation and those blacks who were descendants of the enslaved. When an African dies, it was the custom that a *Kont* would be "thrown" for him so that his soul would journey peacefully back to the motherland. This religious practice was also confirmed by

Lawrence Jn. Baptiste, a descendant of the *Djiné* people who settled in Vieux Sucrieux, (*Vyé Sikwi*) in the old district of Dauphin, with whom I conducted an interview. Lawrence remembers that during the wake ceremony participants would jump over a container of water to symbolize the return of their souls to Africa.

Victor explains to Lomax and Simmons that as *chantwèl* or *kontè* (Conteur) it was his role to sing the songs during the ritual. Simmons asks Victor how he has managed to remember the songs. Victor answers that they were taught to him by his mother and father. He is not African (as they were) so he holds on to the memory of them (in his head). As his parents are dead he keeps the songs alive. "The elaborateness of funeral rites in the area is cast in terms of the role of the ancestors in the lives of their descendants, and because it is important to have the assurance of ancestral good will, the dead are honored with extended and costly rituals.[8]" When Simmons asks Victor why he likes the songs so much he responds that he does so because he knows that he is descended from Africa. He adds that he will not lose that memory. Victor goes on to explain that African music moves him like no other. He makes a distinction between the practices he learnt from his parents and those that surround him in St. Lucia. He participates in St. Lucian drumming because he knows it but whenever he re-lives the music of his parents, he cries.

The following is a transcription of the interview with Victor followed by an analysis in English:

> **Simmons**: *Misyé-Danm mwen just kay expliché bay zòt sa nou ka fè ouswè-a. Sé byen enpotan. Ou sav tout vyé chanté, vyé dansé, ba'y jan ansyen ka dispawèt. Se jen jan-an apwésan yo enmen rock and roll, tout sa tout sé bay-y sa-a mé sa pa say o, mé sa ki san nou sé pou nou pwésévé'y. Bon sé chanté sa-a nou ka record-yo. Yo ka alé adan an college pou tout sé moun Sent Lisi épi tout sé lézòt péyi sa-a. Bon I byen enpotent pou nou sav manyè sé ba'y sa-a koumansé. Bon koumannyè ou pè di mwen Misyé Victor Kinmannyè ki ou ka chonjé sé chantè sa-a toujou?*

Victor: É sa manman mwen èk papa mwen té moutwé mwen. M'a soti an Afrik, sé sa yo té ka ban mwen. Mwen tjébe'y an tèt mwen. Yo mò alo na wépété'y.

Simmons: *Mé poutjikòz ou enmen yo toujou?*

Victor: Pas mwen sav mwen sòti désan Africhen. Ma ka pèd sa.
Simmons: *Ou paka pèd sa. Epi an lòt chòz. Manman'w ek papa'w sé yo ki mountwé'w chanté, se dansé sa-a?*
Victor: Wi.
Simmons: *Bon ès ou ka santi pyes . . . le ou ka lè ou ka lè ou tann an tanbou sa I ka fè an tjè'w.*

Victor: I ka bwennen mwen dépi sé tanbou Africhen, Na chonjé péyi manman-mwen. I ka bwenen mwen.

Simmons: *Me lòt tanbou paka bwenen'w I paha chofé'w?*
Si e pa lòt tanbou masa enbété kon mwen pou li me pis sé li mwen konnèt ki isi Sent Lisi na jwé adan'y me sa manman mwen-an, lè mwen chonjé'y èk papa-mwen na chanté'y èk n'a pléwé.

Other Voice: *Ou paka kopwan sé lòt—la mé ou ka kopwann Africhen boss.*

Simmons: *Zòt ka kowpwann sa ou paka kopwan sé lezòt-la. Bon an lòt chòz. Di mwen. Ki moun ki moutwé'w sa sé mo sa-a an Africhen sa mean.*

Victor: *Papa-mwen.*

Simmons: *Papa'w. Li ki moutwé'w sa sé mo sa-a ka mean? Powyé katumba-a ou kay chanté. I di'w ki sé le moun yo té eslav, yo té sòti Afwik an Afwik adan an batiman. Pwomyé fwa yo wè solèy epi non pa sòlèy syèl lanmè non yo té ka wè syèl avan, mé le yo we glo lanmè bon lè yo wè syèl tousèl yo té sipwis ko yo ka alé yo paté mèm sav ko yo té ka alé. Bon yo dékouvè ki yo té kwè ki sé yo tousèl abò batiman-an ki té ka kopwan langaj yo yo mèm mé manjé-a yo té ka bayo a yo paté satisfè épi'y. Kalté manjé-a* *yo pa té habitwé épi sa bon lè yonn sé moun-an ta ka palé, yo twouvé yon moun, an dokté abò, ki té . . .*

Simmons : *Kisa dòktè-a fè, di mwen.*

Victor*: Lè yo pwan pawòl-a doktè-a wéponn.*

Simmons*: Uh hum . . . Sa dòktè—a wéponn?*

Victor*: I mandé yo, sa yo vlé. Ki say o vlé, pou yo manjé? Yo weponn pistach oben pwa. Sé sa yo té konnèt.*

Simmons*: Mé pistach sé ki sa ann Afwik?*

Victor*: Oben pwa*

Simmons*: Non ann Afwik?*

Victor*: Ann Afwik.*

Simmons*: Non . . . non pistach-la.*
Victor*: Gumba*

Simmons*: Gumba. Èk pwa-a sé kisa*

Victor*: Kasa.*

Simmons*: Kasa. Bon poutji wéson ou ka ni an Koutumba lè an moun mo tousèl. Anfin pa lè an moun mò, mé ou sav lè ou ni lavéhé ou ka ni Katumba? Sa sé an lakoutim?*

Victor*: Wi sa sé lavéhé Afwichen?*

Simmons*: Lavéhé Afwichen. Sé sèl lè ou ka dansé Katumba sé lè ou ni an véhé?*

Victor*: Nou ka dansé Koutumba tout lè mé lè i ni an lanmò nou ni kont nou ka vwéhé bay Afwichen. Fè sav ki mò sa-a I alé. Ek I ni wéjin-li Bondyé ki pwen'y.*

Lomax: *Have you asked him what would happen if they didn't sing Katumba . . . you know what exactly . . .*

Simmons: *Not yet no. Mi. Am sa té kay fèt si on on Nèg Giné. Ou sé kisa Giné enben Kongo?*

Victor: *Kongo èk Giné sé menm i ka vini misyé.*

Simmons: *Vwé?*

Victor: *Sé sa ki fèt Sent Lisi yo ka kwiyé nou Kongo. Mé Djiné sé Afwichen sòti an L'Afrique. Kon i wivé isya I fè nou alò. Moun kwiyé nou Kongo.*

Simmons: *Bon si I té ni an Djiné enben an Kongo, an kamawad ou mò èk ou pa ni yon Katumba sa ti té ka fèt?*

Victor: *Si yo ka fè'y yo ka fè'y. Si yo pasa fè'y. I pa ni si i pa ni li Afwichen ki konnèt li pou fè'y, yo ka joué kont kwéyol kon nou habitwé, me si sé an Afwichen ki fè'y nou ka vwéhé, sa'k Afrwichen kopwann li sa ki paka kopwann-li le nou ka jwé'y.*

Simmons: *Bon di mwen am . . . sé jenn jan-an. Es ich-ou, eben ti ich-ou ka pwan pyès lentéwé an sé . . . am, asou sé ba 'hay sa-a, sé bahay jen ansyen zafè dansé avèk tambou katumba tout sa?*

Victor: *Misyé memsi yo paka kopwann li yo désolé adan'y.*

Simmons: *Yo désolé adan. (laughter)*

Victor : *Yo paka kopwann-li mé le yo tann tanbou-a yo an man'y.*

Simmons: *Alòs . . . alòs san pli fò pasé glo. Pa menm wòm ki ka pli fò pasé san.*

Victor: *Yo désolé lè yo tann li.*

Simmons: *Yo désolé, wi.*[9]

In the interview above, Simmons explains the objective of the project to the participants. St. Lucian folk music and folk dances were under threat since St. Lucians were showing a growing interest in music like rock and roll and other kinds of music that were not their own. Simmons tells that what is ours we need to preserve and for this reason the party will be documenting the folk culture for a college in the states for all St. Lucians so that it can be shared as well with other countries. As an aside I would like to make the point that fifty years since Simmons spoke those words, the evidence of the usefulness of the Lomax project sounds a ring of truth to his declaration.

After his declaration Simmons proceeds to ask Victor how he has managed to remember the songs. Victor answers that they were taught to him by his mother and father. He is not African (as they were) so he holds on to the memory (in his head). As his parents are dead he keeps the song alive. When Simmons asks him why he likes the songs so much he responds that he does because he knows that he is descended from Africa. He adds that he will not lose that memory. Victor goes on to explain that African music moves him like no other. He makes a distinction between the practices he learnt from his parents and those that surrounded him in St. Lucia. He participates in St. Lucian drumming because he knows it but whenever he re-lives the music of his parents he cries.

Victor remembers the stories that his parents told him of their travels on sea from Africa to the Caribbean. They told him how long they stayed before seeing any sunlight, the times when they could only see sky then only sea and sky. They had no idea where they were being taken. They told him of an incident when they complained openly of the food which they didn't like and became very surprised when someone, a doctor understood them and asked him what they liked. They told him that they liked Gumba, their word for peanuts and *Kasa* (peas).

In response to his questions about the purpose and origins of the Koutumba, Victor states that Koutumba is an African form of the wake. He explains that they have Koutumba regularly but particularly when an African dies, they throw a Kont for him. When someone dies if there is someone who knows how to do it exactly as the Giné do then it is done that way but if not the Kont is thrown the Creole way that they are accustomed to. Victor dismisses the distinction between a Giné and a Kongo. According to him, Giné refers to those who were born in Africa but those who were born in St. Lucia are called Kongo. When Simmons asks Victor whether his children and grandchildren show an interest in the *Kont*, he responds that even if they do not understand it they are totally enraptured by the form.

Gilroy writes that "the distinctive language of identity appears again when people seek to calculate how tacit belonging to a group or community can be transformed into more active styles of solidarity, when they debate where the boundaries around a group should be constituted and how-if at all-they should be enforced.[10]" The significance of Victor's responses to Simmons is that there was an ease of interaction between African immigrant culture and that of the descendants of the enslaved.

Victor is certainly an example of the intersection of two worlds, that of the African immigrants, his direct ancestry and that of the descendants of the enslaved into whose society he was born. His allegiance to his ancestral roots is as clear and strong as his commitment to continuing the ritual practices that his parents passed on to him. In his own words he holds in his head *"mwen tjébe'y an tèt mwen"*, in his memory, the African derived cultural practices because they reflect his roots which he refuses to lose. Thus Victor is a highly important as an agent of continuity of African cultural practices, not only among his generation but also among the generation of his offspring. His description of the response of his children to the African rituals, that, even though they did not understand the words, *"yo désolé adan'y"* expresses simultaneously, the strength of his satisfaction as well as the depth of involvement of the children in the practices.

It is apparent however that the descendants of the enslaved also practiced a Kont akin to that of the immigrants. This becomes evident from Victor's explanation that *"si i pa ni li Afwichen ki konnèt li pou fè'y, yo ka joué kont kwéyòl kon nou habitwé"*, meaning, that in the event that there was no African to perform the Koutumba, they would, as they were accustomed to, throw a Kont in Kwéyòl. Invariably the wakes would involve the sharing of stories, jokes, riddles that referred to actual incidents that happened in the community. Among the songs recorded by Lomax and Simmons are some which contain African lexicon but many others are completely in Kwéyòl. The following some examples that I have transcribed:

Lendi apwémidi Manko Kline tonbé malad
Vwéhé aché dokte pou bali leximansyon
Le labé-a vini sékula sécularom
I kwe sé wom i di misye labe, ban mwen san glo

Misyé labé
Ban mwen san mwen sa glo[11]
Misyé labé
Ban mwen san mwen san glo
Misyé labe
Ban mwen san mwen san glo

The *Kont* above tells the story of an individual Manko Kline who fell very ill. The doctor was called in to give her "leximasyon" and the priest to administer the last rites. As the priest arrived with the libation, Manko Kline mistook the substance for rum and asked the priest to give her hers without water. In another example which follows, the story is told of a father who had a growing daughter, sufficiently developed that the father would send her to sell milk. Often she would meet an old man who would speak with her but she would respond negatively. One day a cow on the loose begun chasing her and she had no choice but to seek refuge at the old man's house. When the old man came home, he uttered *lalay ti bay* and she responded *bay sa*. He uttered *lalay ti bay*, and she responded *bay sa*. Here is the story:

Kwik kwak kwik kwak

Enben Manmay-la sa ou kwè ki té di sa. Sa sé té ni yon Papa ki té ni yon fi. Fi-a té fi tèlman i té ka vwéhé'y poté lèt. An vyéko ka jwen li. Lè vyéko-a ka jwen li vyéko-a ka palé ba li i ka di non. Vyéko-a pasé I paka kopwan ék vyéko-a. An jou bèf mawon pati dèhè'y. Lè i pati dèhè'y i di sé laky vyéko I ni pou twapé'y. Kwik kwak. Lè vyéko-a wivé misyé. Vyéko-a di lalaytiby, I di bay sa . . .

Lalaytibay
Bay sa
Lalaytibay
Bay sa
Lalytibay
Bay sa
Lalaytibay
Bay sa
Lalaytibay
Bay sa
I bay
Bay sa

I bay
Bay sa
I bay
Bay sa
I bay
I bayyyyyyyyy.[12] (general laughter)

The storytellers at wakes were usually men who would travel in a group and keep the yard alive. Not only were the stories reflective of events that transpired in the community but the form rendered them highly interactive. The group would bond in the artistic experience while thrashing out issues relevant to their space for "identity is always bounded and particular."

In order to gain more insight into the form of the *Kont*, I spoke with several elderly persons in the old district of Dauphin. Gilbert Joseph, a gentleman of Labonne in his late seventies who as a young man was one of the community's pall bearers, confirmed that there were two separate periods when the *Kont* was performed. One of them was the *Kont Lanmò* (Conte La Mort) which referred to the wake ceremony held on the night after the burial of the deceased and the other was *Kont an mwa Novam* (Kont in November) which coincided with *mwa létousen*, (Mois Les Tous Saints) the ceremonies of All Saints Day and All Souls Day.

KONT LANMÒ

Miss Angelie Norley, a farmer and a community leader told me much about the *Kont Lanmò*. Those were the days before the establishment of funeral homes. The body would be bathed with alcohol, rolled over and shaken to rid it of any waste that would have been near release. Usually burials would take place the same day of the passing. However if the death happens too late during the day then the body would be kept until the next day. Those were also the days before most people had radios sets, so death announcements were done by sounding of a conch shell. In the first instance, the conch shell is blown three times to indicate that someone has passed and that the pall bearers should come to the house. It is sounded three times again to indicate to the community that they should come out of their homes to give support as the body would be taken out of the house for the journey to the cemetery. The conch shell would be sounded a final three times at the point when the body is actually leaving the house.

After the body is taken out of the house, the mattress would be put out to sun and cleaned. The clothes of the deceased would be taken out by the women to be washed. This washing would take place at the point where the river meets the sea. On the day that the body was taken out to the cemetery, it was a big event. Transportation was not readily available so the custom would be to carry the body manually to the cemetery. The body would be carried in a hammock made out of a thick cloth, the sides of which were fastened around two bamboo poles. Several barebacked men alternated in twos, one in front and the other behind, the poles resting on their shoulders. People stood by the side of the road to bid farewell to the departed. Once the deceased had been buried, extended family and friends kept company with the grieving family but entertainment happened only on the night of the burial and on *denyé vèy-la* (la dernière veille), eight nights after the burial. On the night after the burial, family and friends would keep vigil in the household of the deceased praying with the rosary, singing various catholic hymns and other songs of mourning, many of which were in French Creole. During this time lots of coffee would be served, rum would also be available as well as simple eats such as bakes and cassava. On the final night however, there would be a feast. Members of the community would assist in the provision and preparation of food and drink. Storytellers would remain outside and keep the yard alive. Ring games and riddles would also be popular during this time. Thus on that eighth night the grief of the passing really becomes overshadowed by a lively atmosphere and this would become heightened when the community's griot *threw a Kont* for the deceased.

KONT NOVANM

Anton "Ananj" Marius, a seventy two year old farmer and accomplished dancer from Labonne, spoke to me about the second type of *Kont*, the one that took place in November. As a very young man, Anton walked from Labonne to Derameau to the yard of Misilia, now deceased, of Derrameau up Morne Citron. This was the most popular space in the North where the event used to take place. I journeyed to the site that Anton spoke of and I was absolutely fascinated. Misilia's compound where her granddaughter now resides is situated on the crest of the hill where one has a clear view of the

La Souciere, the most spectacular mountain in the north. *La Sourciere* is the source of water but also the fount of folklore and mythology. It was the inspiration for the home of *Makak,* the central character in Walcott's most famous play, *"Dream on Monkey Mountain".* It is said that the *Djiné* people settled within sight of this mountain as it served as constant reminder of their homeland in Africa.

Misilia's yard also overlooked the entire plantation of Marquis Estate, at one time the largest slave plantation on the island. Hundreds of Africans were imported to work on this estate after emancipation. Misilia hosted the *Kont* in at this vantage point where there was also a constant breeze coming from the Atlantic. It is little wonder that the event was also referred to as "Belair Conte"; bel-air, meaning good air, fresh breeze. Misilia, had a stove oven and a *platin* to the back of the yard where she served freshly baked creole loaves as well as fresh cassava to her gathering. She also sold *Malcochon,* that good old strong white rum. Folk came from all the surrounding communities to dance. The *Kont* would be a story, a short satirical anecdote, about an incident of interest which evoked fun and laughter. No names would be mentioned and much use was made of symbol, metaphor and animal characters and done so skillfully that those gathered would know who was being referred to. Songs of the *Kont* often narrated some aspect of the life of a member of the community or some significant event that went against the norms of the community such as incest, domestic violence or theft. The *chantwel* was usually a man and his chorus was usually made up of women. After the story, the *chantwel* in the typical African call and response pattern would throw his song and receive a response from the chorus. The mood is often celebratory and this mood is enhanced by the vigourous drumming and dancing which follows. Anton gave me a description of the dances. He likened the dance to that of the Quadrille. As Anton put it, violin played the quadrille, but the tanbou (drum) played the *Kont.* *"Ou ni pou plasé'y menm kon Kwadjril.* (You had to set it just like Quadrille) The dancers had to place themselves, had to be set; there was form, just as in Quadrille. Four couples led the dance. *Kat danm èk kat kavalyé,* (quatres dames et quatres cavaliers) meaning that there would four women and four men, eight dancers at any one time in the space. If one thinks of the four cardinal points and places each couple on one of the points then one would visualize the structure. Man and woman from opposite sides would meet in the centre of the space, dance, then continue across as they replaced each other on the rim. Dance in *Kont* involves much demonstration of prowess and sexual play.

The *Kont* has several variations that allows for much improvisation and freedom within the space. There is *Kont Anlè* and *Kont Atè* as well as the Bèlè Kont. I was fortunate to have these dances demonstrated to me by "Kawo" the *Kontè* of the Secret Band. In the *Kont Anlè*, literally meaning 'Kont Above", one dances into the space, raising each leg alternatively, while balancing gracefully with the arms. In the *Kont Atè* literally meaning 'Kont on the gound" one dances into the space, with the back of the hands at the waist and each leg moving back and forth remaining close to the ground, toes to the front and heel to the back. In the *Bèlè Kont*, a female dancer waltzes into the space holding the tips of a long wide skirt, a version which developed for the performance of women on the stage perhaps, in which there may actually be more than one woman performing. In this version the female may sing while coming in, stop, tell her story then revert to the singing and dancing.

The *Kont* therefore is about narrative expressed with the use more than one artform. It is a form in which individuals are allowed to claim the space within the circle of the audience and express their individuality. Yet the *Kont* also facilitates a dance and a cementing of camaraderie between couples, male as well as female. One male may join the other into the space in the *"Kont Alè"* and then they would both part, leaving the space for an incoming dancer. Predominantly though the space makes allowances for the "courtship' of male and female. Typically, after a male or female dancer enters in flair and display, they would attract a member of the opposite sex to join them into the space. This would be followed by very intricate dialogic footwork between male and female and a tease and test of skill and prowess which expectantly came to a climax with the *blotjé*, the bounce of one pelvis against another to a sudden but predictable lash of the drum and the sounds of applause from the community. Thus during this period of Roman Catholic's All Souls Day when death is commemorated, there is a celebration of the fertility and continuity of life. By the first week of December when the *Kont* comes to an end the community is well unto preparations for celebrations of Christmas.

KÈLÈ

The *Kélé* ceremony which was practiced in the old French district of Dauphin in St. Lucia among nineteenth century African immigrants and subsequently their descendants was a highly organized event to give thanks to the gods, Ogun and Shango for a good harvest. The *Kélé* was a highly ritualized practice and was sustained by the kinship among a group who referred to themselves as the *"Neg Djiné"*, meaning, literally, Blacks of Guinea. Kremser notes that the *"Kele-cult is of special importance for cultural scientists and ethnographers with a special interest in African and Afro-American themes. In contrast to most other creole folk traditions, the Kele-cult has remained a nearly pure*

African tradition over the past 100 years since it was first reported in St. Lucia."[13]

According to Harold Simmons, the Kele ceremony "began in about 1867, shortly after the arrival of families from Western Nigeria, of the Ekiti tribe, 20 years after the abolition of slavery."[14] Simmons also reports that:

> "A *Kèlè* usually takes place usually on the first Sunday in the New Year, August, October, the Sunday before Lent, the First Sunday after Easter and the last Sunday in November. It may be held to ask the ancestors to intercede for a successful future, good crops, thanksgiving for a good harvest, intercession for an acquittal in an impending trial which strange to relate was withdrawn by the police), or it may be that one person may have had a dream or a vision of his dead parents who asked that a memorial service be held.[15]"

A significant element of the *Kèlè* ceremony was the slaying of a sheep and the drinking of its blood by the high priest and members of his clan. Kremser reports that the African deities of Shango and Ogun play an integral role in the Kele. "Shango"-stones ("Wa Shango" =thunder stones) are at the heart of several religious practices of the "djine". They are used in many different ways . . . since they are also used for curing certain illnesses, protecting one's house from fire, and for safeguarding one's journey." [16]

However Kremser also states that:

> "Whereas "Shango"-stones are conceived as being the material representation of god, the deity addressed in most prayers during a Kele ceremony is "Ogun".

"ESHU" The name of "Eshu" or "Akeshew" is sometimes associated with the calabash which contains all sorts of things, some of them are of a secret nature. It is always smashed at the end of the ceremony, whereby the person, performing an acrobatic dance, will throw it toward the West.[17]"

The practise of the *Kèlè* ritual like other African derived religious practices on the island was condemned by the Catholic Church as a practice of evil and as a result had to be practiced secretly. It is significant that the stones used in the *Kèlè* ceremony are placed on the altar in the form of a cross and several cross signs are made upon the raw yams before it is placed in Olive oil. The cross is a dominant symbol of Catholicism. Were these catholic elements that crept into the tradition?

Of crucial significance to present day cultural forms in St. Lucia, is the drumming and dancing that immediately succeeds the ritual of the *Kèlè* and the role of these practices in sustaining a sense of community and group identity. Even though the *Kèlè* ritual is no longer practised, many of the cultural groups which arose in the rural communities of old Dauphin, still practice the drumming and dances that were associated with the old African ceremony.

MASQUERADE

Warner-Lewis writes that "Masking was an integral part of West African religious culture, intimately connected with secret societies.[18]"

Carnival, up till recently in the islands of Trinidad, and St. Lucia, were synonymous with the wearing of masks and the idea of "playin mas" is derived from the practice of wearing a mask at carnival time. Warner Lewis observes that "From the late eighteenth century there have been written reports of masking by Africans in various parts of the Caribbean . . . [19]"

During the season of Christmas and New Year celebrations, festivals in the Caribbean seem to reach their pinnacle, partly because there was an apparent license for public display. Apart from the custom of serenade (known as Sewénal in St. Lucia) where groups of drummers and singers moved around entering various households in the community, there were also street masquerades. The Christmas festive season:

> became yet another time for engaging in African festival-like activity: organizing groups of masqueraders, outfitting them with costumes, making and tuning musical instruments, rehearsing traditional and original compositions, and engaging in public expressions of gaiety, abandon, satire, and cynicism for at least once a year[20].

The masquerade in St. Lucia that I witnessed as a child were manifested in three forms and all took place on separate occasions during the latter part of the year culminating as it were during the Christmas season. The Flower Festivals of La Rose and La Marguerite festival was celebrated on the 30th of August and the 17th of October respectively. Papa Diable on Christmas day and *Pay Banann* on New Year's Day

These forms of masquerade, the Flower Festivals, the Pay Banann and Papa Diable, similar to the other traditions of masquerade found in many other Caribbean territories speak of the political suaveness of the oppressed descendants of Africa. Bettelheim writes that there is evidence that in Jamaica, "masked and costumed performers have paraded the streets at Christmas"[21]. Of the Jamaican festival she found that the "street performances included both masked characters performing in mime as well as troupes of players acting out scenes from English theatrical plays.[22]" The masked characters wore colourful costumes, horned headdresses, portraying characters such as the cowhead, the horsehead, the devil, pitchy patchy. Bettelheim also writes of the British influences on the masquerades and believes that "the concept that all (Jonnkunnu) festivals are related through British colonialism is not unreasonable given the substantial trade that occurred among the British islands"[23]. It appears that integral to the development of the masquerade in Jamaica was the organization of competitions among masquerade groups.

> The competitions highlighted two different styles. Some included kings, queens, bishops, and courtiers-representaions

of an early modern Europe. Some troupes performed
European dances. Other troupes, however, demonstrated a
strong African influence. Their performance style and the
importance of animal characters recalled a powerful African
aesthetic[24].

There are marked similarities in Bettelheim's description of
masquerade in Jamaica, and that of St. Lucia which not only point to
their common origin but also reveal how there was a deliberate policy
among the plantocracy to encourage rivalry among groups.

In addition to the ritual of the *Papa Djab*, there were other
manifestations of masquerade in the city. Public celebrations
during the Christmas festive season in Saint Lucia were divided
into two segments. Celebrations took place in the weeks leading
up to Christmas. It was during this period immediately before
Christmas that *Papa Diable* took over the city. The second segment of
celebrations began on New Year's Eve when the city came alive for the
traditional fair on the then Columbus Square[25] and preparations for
Old Year's Mass in the Roman Catholic Church. It was during this
second segment that the other masquerade characters invaded the city
with the performances. Such characters went by the names, *Uncle Sam,
Mary Ancet*, and *Chouval Bwa*. Another set of characters were the *Pay
Banann* who were dressed in costume, made up of strips of dry banana
leaves, or bits of colourful cloth decorated with mirrors, a headdress
with feathers or horns and grass skirts, their faces also smeared with
a black substance like paint or molasses. These were a group of male
performers who would occupy a space on the then Columbus Square,
near the Roman Catholic Cathedral, where the annual fair was held
to mark New Year's Day. Accompanied by the music of a flutist, and a
couple of drummers, one of which played the kettle drum, these men
danced vigorously to the music of fife and drum, and in the process,
to the delight of a circle of onlookers, showed off strong hairy legs
beneath their skirts. They came in the morning before the fair actually
commenced and soon after the morning mass, to occupy a corner of
the Square on the pavement. This was somewhat out of the way of the
officially designated booths where the brown creoles would be selling
local delicacies to families, particularly children. The *Pay Banann*

dancers were extremely conspicuous and attracted crowds of children and adults who threw coins unto a mat spread out on the pavement before them. The annual fair was organized by the brown middle class of the city of Castries and despite the fact that many of them would be of French ancestry, Castries in this post emancipation era, was the centre of British hegemony and the English language and culture were the acceptable forms of expression. Thus the very performance of the *Pay Banann* dancers on the city square near the Roman Catholic Cathedral was of tremendous political significance.

Having wrenched permission from the white commercial class to attempt some grassroots merchandising during the holiday season, the brown middle class left a corner space for their lesser black brothers. The annual fair, however temporary, became a significant disruption of the social system—a dislocation of the colonial spatial configurations. As the cyclical rhythm of the event ensured a place for *Pay Bannan*, their performances and the presence of their supporters became further justified. *Pay Bannan* was not only a literal encroachment unto the colonial space it was also a serious invasion of the colonial discourse. The statement was that cultural practices of the black folk and those whom those practices represented had a place in entire society. There were also elements of satire in *Pay Bannan*. At a time when the Catholic ladies of the Victorian era were decently dressed in their pretty frocks, the *Pay Bannan* dancers were moving vigorously with interjections of sensual gimmicks to invoke laughter from their supporters. Even though some frowned upon the dances, considering them improper, the very sight of a band of cross-dressed men raising their skirts to show off legs, shaking their padded behinds, bending, all to the infectious rhythms of the masquerade music proved to be sheer delight for many. After the masquerade, all who came to the fair including those who frowned upon the activity interacted as one and walked the perimeter of the Square sharing and negotiating the space, *interrelating*, while they patronized the various stalls.

SOLO

The *Solo*, another popular community art form practiced in October and still alive in areas such as Monchy, Babonneau and Aux Leon, Dennery, may very likely be a more secular development of the arts from the *Kèlè*, *Kont* and the *Koutumba*. In Monchy, *Solo* as performed by the Secret Band also draws on the arts associated with the *Koudmen(The Pitchay)*. The *Solo* form comprises singers and dancers accompanied by the music of the drums, the *chac-chac*[26], and the *Ti bwa*[27]. The singing follows a call and response pattern with the chantwelle/chantwel taking the lead and the chorus of women responding as they dance around in a circular fashion. The *Kont* and the *Solo* are fitting examples of how art forms directly derived from Afro Creole religious practices still function to facilitate expression, communion and group dynamism.

Thus these continuities that I have identified can be perceived as offshoots of religious ceremonies carried over from Africa that became modified in response to New World dynamics. Elements of the the *Kèlè*, and *Koutumba* ceremonies were carried over by nineteenth century African immigrants causing another infusion of African religious practices in the Caribbean. Warner Lewis supports the view that the Yoruba were "able to make a distinct imprint on the African/French/English synthesis which constituted Creole culture both at that time (of their immigration) and well into the twentieth century . . ." She believes that the "similarity between certain Yoruba and Asian institutions then served to make Creole culture a more favourable avenue for inter-racial cultural synthesis. Olmos Fernendez and Gebert-Paravisini attribute the "persistence and predominance of Yoruba worship" in Caribbean religious practices to "the creation of a complex Yoruban religious structure prior to their arrival in the New World, and to their having been the most massive of all African groups, which allowed them to replenish and strengthen African transplanted culture.[28]"

Thus although African religious practices may not have survived intact in the Caribbean to this day, there are many cultural practices which functioned to maintain and consolidate group identity. African immigrants who settled in the Caribbean became part of a society that was already creolized. The Christian theocracy imposed by the colonial culture was re-interpreted within the Yoruban Orisha festivals. Even when participating in Church activities which honoured Christian saints, Africans were paying homage to their own gods such as Ogun and Shango. The rituals of the Kont and Solo are extremely important for the practice of the community arts and for the inculcation of a sense of psychosocial security among members of the community. It is this solidarity that would empower the descendants of Africans to adapt other ritualistic traditions such as the various forms of masquerade from the Yoruban Egungun festivals, for specific performances meant to infiltrate then displace the racist discourse in the urban colonial space.

THE FLOWER SOCIETIES

Evidence of the existence of the The Flower Societies, La Rose and La Marguerite(Lawòz èk Lamagwit), suggests that they existed in St. Lucia as far back as the mid nineteenth century. Several letters to the editor of the Voice Newspaper during that period describe the social impact of these societies on nineteenth century St. Lucia.[29] There may be a direct correlation between the colonial management of nineteenth century African immigrants and the development of the Flower Societies. Some information by Olmos and Paravisini-Gebert on the impact of catholic influenced social structures on nineteenth century Caribbean society may also shed some light here. The influx of African immigrants into the Caribbean after emancipation would have caused resurgence in African religious and cultural expressions in the region. As a result these free immigrants would have experienced a degree of social snobbery from the creole population. Writing of Cuba, these writers state that freemen "discovered a refuge from the oppressive racism of the larger society in their clubs and fraternal organizations formed on the basis of ethnic origins, where they could maintain their religious values and sustain themselves through their remembrance of cultures of origin.[30]" The church sponsored brotherhoods "in which groups gathered to assist one another in times of need and to worship their patron saint.[31]" Some of Olmos and Paravisini-Gebert's writing on the Cuban nineteenth mutual aid confraternities is worth quoting in full as it so aptly describes certain features of the flower societies:

"Excluded from white fraternities, blacks were permitted to govern and organize their own institutions that were a combination of a mutual aid society and a social confraternity to plan the communal feasts, dances, and carnival processions and help members in need. Each cabildo had a house, frequently owned by the members, and the money they collected helped to finance their activities, assist members in need, pay for burials and occasionally purchase a member's freedom.[32]" In St. Lucia the equivalent of the cabildos were the accommodation provided by the Friendly Society Halls where the La Rose and La Maguerites met and practiced. These organizations of free Africans reflected a strategy by the colonial authorities to encourage those practices that "could be reinterpreted within the church and radically opposing those that could not.[33]" Significantly though, despite the apparent strategic management of the Africans by the colonialists, the St. Lucian Flower Festivals has been an instrument through which these Africans have been able to consolidate their talents and infiltrate the discourse of colonial society. As Gilroy puts it, "Identity becomes a question of power and authority when a group seeks to realize itself in a political form.[34]" The Flower Festivals of La Rose and La Maguerite, (*Lawòz* èk *Lamagwit*) are an example of how the descendants of Africans have adapted the theatre of the West African masquerade tradition to engage the attention of the colonial authorities. Before discussing the political implications of the Flower Societies however, it is important to examine their structure and form. Anthony offers a description of the Flower Festivals:

The structure of these two societies would seem to indicate something of their function within colonial society. Both groups are hierarchically structured with a king and queen as head of each society and other dignitaries patterned upon the socioeconomic structure of colonial society. Thus, after the king and queen came princes and princesses[35].

While the highlight on the festival is the carnival like parades through the urban space and the performances at Government House etc, it is important to note that the actual preparations for the festival begin much earlier. There is a marked contrast in the structure of the activities during the preparations for the festival and the actual masquerade itself. Further Anthony describes that:

> preparations for the respective La Rose and La Maguerite festivals begin several months before the actual feast days. Each group would rent a hall and particularly on weekends hold séances. These consist of all night singing and dancing where drinks are sold and various games played. The central figure at the séance is the chantwell who sustains the tenor and spirit of the evening's entertainment. The song and dance types associated with La Rose and La Marguerite are many. There is much more variation and spontaneity at séances than at the grand fete when the significance of the occasion demands more discipline. At a séance, one can witness anything from a "Mapa" to a "Quibishe" although the former, a kind of "Gwan Won" is the most popular at séances[36].

In the Flower Festivals members of La Rose and La Marguerite costume themselves in red/pink and white, and blue and white respectively, then parade around the community paying homage to their respective saints. Thus aspects of the festivals which were for open public display were structured like European ceremonial marches but once the Africans reached the privacy of their yards and sheds, they engaged fully in their exuberant expressions of drumming, dancing and revelry with the free use of alcohol for the liberation of their spirits.

Interestingly Abrahams et tal, have found evidence in an extract from Beckford of a similar feature in Jamaica where "negroes" from neighbouring estates are divided into distinct parties, "some call themselves blue girls, and some red: and their clothes are generally characteristic of their attachment.[37]" It is quite remarkable is the fact that in both islands the colours of red and blue are used to represent different parties. In the same *Extract of the Extracts* by Abraham et tal, one anonymous writer in 1797, writes that "The negroes from the different districts in Guinea associate in parties and wander about the town, diverting themselves with their own peculiar singing, instruments, and dances, the last of which they stop to perform.[38]" Here is yet another confirmation of the link of the form of the masquerade to the African region of Guinea. Of course these European writers from whose writings those extracts were selected by Abraham et tal betray the ignorance of Europeans of the rationale of African cultural practices as well as their absolute racism in their condescension. Breen who writes of the St. Lucian Flower Festivals is a major culprit in that regard. From Breen's perception, participants of the flower festivals were simply "aping those above them in finery and dress" and their divisions into societies were simply to "gratify their propensity for dancing"[39]. Breen does recognize though the political elements of the Festivals, that "at one period they were invested with a political character; and their occasional allusions to English and French, Republicans and Bonapartists would seem to confirm this impression"[40]. His analysis though is so coloured by his obvious disdain for the "negroes" however, as he refers to the descendants of Africans that he does not reveal any understanding of the identity politics inherent in the practice of the rituals. Thus as far as he is concerned the festivals "connection with politics must have ceased at the termination of the struggle between England and France . . . [41]"

I would like to suggest that while on the surface, members of the Flower Festivals appeared to be simply dancing and singing and representing catholic saints, the practices were in fact driven by the need of these descendants of Africans to maintain their identity in the most practical way that they knew, which is to carry on the teachings and practices of their ancestors. The continuity of these traditions was ensured not in the parade through the streets, but during the preparations leading up to the festival, when the community would bond, when the narratives would be re-called, when the stories, the songs, the drum patterns, the dances, would be re-enacted and when the strict adherence to form would respectfully invite the ancestral spirits into the gathering and through their re-entrance, the community would joyfully cement their ties and celebrate again and again, their sense of belonging, celebrate in effect, their identity.

Thus the Flower festivals have in all practical purposes functioned as political groups. They harness collective talents to engage those in power and authority and to claim a space within the broader society without breaking allegiance to their ancestry; without giving up their identity. There is a song from the La Rose Festival which reflects the awareness of the practitioners that their very survival rests upon the collective energies of their *movement*. The song goes:

Ay ya yay manmay la woz
Ay ya yay manmay la woz
Ay ya yay manmay la woz
Si nou pa bwiyé nou kay mò.

Which translates as:

Oh children of La Rose
Oh children of La Rose
Oh children of La Rose
If we don't move we'll surely die.

For the practical recitation of the song I have translated the word *bwiyé* as move but it is difficult to translate this concept into one word. For *bwiyé* in Creole does suggest movement but is also suggests shine, coming from the French *briller* which means to shine. Thus in effect, the term *bwiyé* means to make oneself stand out through action, that is, to make an impact. The song functions as a rallying cry to members of the group that if this is not achieved they will die. Death of the movement means death of their spirit, death of their identity. Unless their songs flourish, unless their movement stands out, unless they are brilliant in their costume and performance, then they are as good as dead because the whole objective of the masquerade is to claim a space, to stamp their relevance on the platforms of the official discourse. Thus leaders were in positions to negotiate with holders of the highest offices of the colonial hierarchy. The priest solicited their assistance for church building and church restoration projects, the governor general and prime minister welcomed their performances into their official residences. Ordinary peasants they were but their identities became known, their skills respected but even more importantly by wearing the garb of some of the most revered occupations in the society, they made a statement that they were equal in capacity.

PAPA DJAB

This other form of masquerade also took place during the Christmas festive season and was led by the figure of *Papa Djab*. (Papa

Diable, Father Devil) *Papa Djab* was dressed in a long red overall, wore a long white beard, and carried a long stick which ended in a spread of thongs shaped like toes. This highly conspicuous figure was followed by a chorus of young men dressed in shorts, their bodies painted in black who danced in the streets and responded with chants to the call of *Papa Djab*. On Christmas day, during the time of the major catholic mass, *Papa Djab* and his imps would travel from as far as Soufriere into the city and to terrorize and entertain the youth. The highlight of this performance however was an elaborate ritual of death and resurrection, undoubtedly a parody of the Christian story of death and resurrection. The basic chants of *Papa Djab* were as follows:

> Woy Woy
> *Mi jab–la!*
> Woy Woy
> *Mi jab–la!*
> Woy Woy
> *Mi jab–la!*
>
> Ki lè i yé
> *Hi gas!*
> Ki le i yé
> *Hi gas!*
>
> Woy Woy
> *Mary ansèt!*
> Woy Woy
> *Mary ansèt!*
> Woy woy
> *Mary ansèt!*
> Mary ka dansé byen hosé
> *Ri ri ha!*
> Mary ka dansé byen hosé
> *Ri ri ha!*
> Mary ka dansé byen hosé
> *Ri ri ha!*
>
> Ki le i yé
> *Hi gas!*

Ki ke i yé
Hi gas!

Ri pokotoy . . . ripokotoy . . . ripokotoy . . . ?
Ri . . . ha!

My translation follows:

Woy Woy
Here's the devil!
Woy Woy
Here's the devil!
Woy Woy
Here's the devil!

What time is it?
Who cares!
What time is it?
Who cares!
What time is it?
Who cares!

Mary high and mighty dances
Ri ri ha!
Mary high and mighty dances
Ri ri ha!
Mary high and mighty dances
Ri ri ha!

What time is it?
Who cares!
What time is it?
Who cares!
What time is it?
Who cares!
Ri pokotoy . . . ripokotoy . . . ripokotoy . . . ?
Ri . . . ha!

Papa Djab and his *Ti Djabs* moved through the city of Castries with their performances. They performed along the streets of the Roman Catholic Church, Columbus Square and within the general perimeter of the city. The brown and white elite of Castries often came out in their balconies looking down in reluctant fascination and amusement at the spectacle. The music and chanting were infectious. This was Christmas when the Roman Catholic priests would be reminding their flock that they should stay away from the devil, a representation of which was fixed at the back of the church for all to see, black, with horns, lying on the ground with an angel holding a spear over him. Thus when *Papa Djab* and his followers marched through the city making this dramatic announcement of the entrance of the devil, the image presented is very close to that presented at the back of the church. Here is the devil in the form of a black man with black followers and the phenotype is emphasized by the black molasses that is totally smeared over their bodies. In colonial times this was an absolutely powerful satirical poke at the racist discourse of the church. *Woy Woy/Mi Djab-la!* Here is the black devil that you have been preaching about! Part of the satirical punch of the ritual was that there was a mixture of consternation and fascination at the character of *Papa Djab*. Children flocked to go near him even if they knew that he would lunge to poke them with his pitchfork. They roared with laughter and had fun joining the responses to the devil chants and imitating the leg movements of the imps. Perhaps part of the reason for the attraction to *Papa Djab* may be that his red costume and long white beard also signified Father Christmas. This duality in the costuming of the character would act as a buffer against any fear of the devil in him.

Papa Djab, may certainly be seen as an attack on the religious doctrines of the church. A recurring theme of Christianity at Christmas time was that Mary, the virgin became pregnant with child by the Holy Ghost because this child was meant to save mankind. Thus Mary is not presented as an ordinary woman with an ordinary pregnancy. However by chanting *Woy Woy/ Mary ancet*, in the streets, Papa Jab again brings a celestial figure down to the earth and reduces the mysticism inherent in the Catholic teachings. In the teachings of the church when Mary became pregnant Joseph hid her away to keep the act a secret. When *Papa Djab* goes chanting in the streets the news that Mary is pregnant, not only is he divulging the secret but he is also reducing Mary's expectancy to an ordinary event with the full sexual insinuations that would accompany the announcement in the community of a woman who surreptitiously becomes pregnant with child. The line that Mary ka *dansé/ byen hosé,* reinforces the satirical poke at the supposed mysticism of Mary's pregnancy. Undoubtedly the accompanied demonstrations of *Mary high and mighty is dancing,* like any one of us black on the streets, is suggestive that Mary is no different from us and enjoys all the sensual pleasures that we too enjoy. Nevertheless Mary's pregnancy is to be celebrated at Christmas time and the chant *Woy Woy/ Mary ancèt,* is absolutely celebratory.

Symbolically the entire performance of *Papa Djab* connects the population of African descendants to the Christian mythology that permeates the religious discourse at Christmas time but also engages the church in a dialogue about its discursive formations of racism. The "elaborate Black Mass of resurrection", a climactic aspect of the ritual where papa jab kills and resurrects the imps on the streets speaks to the syncretistic function of the *Papa Djab* ritual. During this part of the ritual *Papa Djab* kills the imps with his pitch fork then resurrects them. Here Papa Jab is like the high priest of the Kelè, the link between the temporal and the supernatural. He is in fact the high priest of this *black* ritual but here in this role he demonstrates the Christian teachings of the death and resurrection among his followers. As typical of African religious ceremonies though, there is no real distinction between the religious and the secular and thus the form and structure of his demonstration follows the pattern of other African derived masquerades that of the street theatre of the Egungun who gave praise to his ancestral spirits. Symbolically each of the "crucified' black victims on the street are representations of Christ as papa Jab is a representation of the God who bring him back to life.

In assessing the impact of the political intrusion of St. Lucian folk culture including the three forms of masquerades in to the colonial space, one would have to consider the subsequent changes that have transpired in the Roman Catholic Cathedral and the other parishes around the island. The black devil at the back of the Cathedral was first broken by a 'vandal' then taken down completely by church authorities. The music of the church began to include drumming and other African derived rhythms. Dunstan St. Omer, perhaps the islands best known painter, a former student of Harry Simmons, a close personal friend of Walcott since childhood and a staunch Catholic, was commissioned by the church to include locally derived cultural images in the iconography and representations on church walls.

This is the connection that I am making between space and ritual, and between space, ritual and the development of creole forms. As Hall puts it, "now cultural strategies that can make a difference, that's what I'm interested in-those that can make a difference and can shift the dispositions of power"[42]. What I am attempting to describe is the way in which the organization of space was crucial to the cultural practices of the descendants of Africans who continually harnessed power in rustic settings, then actively deepened the creolization of colonial culture by cyclically intruding into its spaces, into its rituals and affecting them, changing them, even while these practices themselves became modified.

The descendants of Africans in St. Lucia and the Caribbean have come quite a long way in ensuring that their representation at all levels of society speak with pride of the strength and beauty of their African heritage. Representation is power and the current discursive formation of a creole culture in St. Lucia embraced by all levels of society developed from a long insidious, persistent trajectory of counter hegemonic representation rooted in the cultural expressions of the folk.

SÈWÉNAL

The Sèwénal refers to a Christmas tradition in which a group of musicians and revelers move around their community playing their instruments and singing while "intruding" into their neighbours' households. Once in the household, they would be greeted with alcohol and food. After entertaining one household they would move unto another.

The Sèwénal has been alive both in the north and south of the island. A group from Ciceron, would leave their community and travel all through Morne Fortune and surrounding areas before descending into Castries. Other groups came from the Trois Piton community. The tradition has also been particularly strong in the various communities near the village of Choiseul such as Daban, Cafeille, Dakiten, Morne Jacques and Belle Vue near Vieux Fort. In the North the practice was also strongly observed in Gros Islet and Castries. Today the Sèwénal is still alive is the communities of Monchy, Mon Repos and Daban.

In Labonne, a small village in the heights of Monchy, the Secret Band meets on Christmas Eve at the house of one of its members and would play drums all throughout the night. A table would be laid with drinks and all through the night pork would be roasted on a grill. At the break of dawn, the drummers, singers and their following would move from "house to house" throughout the community, celebrating the advent of Christmas.

One variation of the Sewénal is the Abwè. Simmons describes this cultural form as a "song-feast" taking place in November and December and practiced only in "the north eastern section of the island, Gros-Islet, the Marquis Valley and Dennery.[43]" According to Simmons, 'participants gather around a long row of tables, on which are saucers of fine salt, peppermint lozenges (called extra strong) or rock mint (called le menthe), bottles of rum and tumblers.[44]" The activity is characterized by the expressions of speeches and songs beginning after the "chantwelle or storyteller sings the verse,[and] the audience joins in the chorus. There is no musical accompaniment, but there is liberal sucking of peppermints and salt (to minimize huskiness in the vocal cords and sipping of white rum, which act is termed in the local creole as "*wuze gorge*" or "*sprinkling of the throat*[45].

Joseph Glasgow, alias French, is a seventy seven year old retired musician of Daban. He lives in a small cottage all by himself in his home community. His children are all overseas and at the time of interview in 2013, it had been six years since his wife passed away. French started participating in the Sèwénal from the time he was about ten years old and through his participation, learnt to practice the banjo, eventually becoming the lead musician. French remembers waking up at 3am to meet with other musicians to play, then starting off again about 8pm until midnight. This he would do every day during the season of the Sèwénal. People prepared for them and on early mornings made them fresh, hot coffee. As a Banjo player French was always in demand and performed at all dances in the community.

French would start playing as early as August or September, not very often though during these months. However the sessions would intensify during the month of November and continue right through the Christmas season. French and his fellow musicians would play all night on Christmas Eve until about 9am at which point they would go their respective homes for breakfast then resume playing again until about 7pm. They would start playing from the top of Daban, reaching all the way to Saltibus, stopping at every household along the way.

Anna Antoine, a Lecturer in Nursing at the Sir Arthur Lewis Community College was also born and raised in the community of Daban still has fond memories of the Sèwénal. Her family has played a leading role in carrying the tradition. Two of her uncles, played the Violin; her elder brother played the Banjo and her cousins played the Chac-Chac and the drum. Sheryl Paul is one of the Chantwelles. Francis Gilliard plays the Banjo. Mrs. Antoine explained that the songs of the Sèwénal are usually based on "some fascinating story" that happened in the community.

Paul Elien, is one of the younger men in the community of Daban who took the tradition of the Sèwénal seriously. Paul started leading the tradition from 1997 and did so until 2010. He played the Cuatro and also functioned as the lead vocalist. Paul learned from the elders in the community such as Mr. French, Selwyn, Mr. Albert and Mr. Kokilo. He was taught to the Cuatro by a man called Long.

Paul speaks with pride of the times when musicians would meet at the top of the hill in Daban and descend, stopping at each house until they arrived at the last one. Then they returned to the centre of the community. Each house would prepare drink and food for the participants, stewed meat, drink etc. According to Paul each household would have something prepared for them, even a jug of coconut water.

Diana Henry, also a Lecturer at the Sir Arthur Lewis Community College was born and raised in La Pointe, Dennery, the home community of Sesenne Descartes. Mrs. Decartes, deceased, was known as Saint Lucia's Queen of Culture. La Pointe is an agricultural community near Mon Repos. Both Communities are part of the village of Micoud.

In La Pointe, the Sèwénal also begins during the months of October-November and lasts till Christmas. The musicians would meet and practice at the home of the leading musician. At the height of the Sèwénal, on Christmas Eve and Christmas Day itself, the musicians take to the streets and would be followed by the people flowing from the various households. They would begin from the bottom of La Pointe and move up to Patience and then go along to Mon Repos. By that time there would be a large following. Musical instruments used for the Sèwénal here are the Baha, the Chac-Chac and the drum.

French the retired musician of Daban, was not pleased with how the custom was observed the year before this interview was conducted. He believed that currently involved begin very late, sometimes on Christmas Eve and he considers the quality of their music quite substandard.

Miss Henry has observed some changes to the Sèwénal in Mon Repos. Whereas in the past, musicians would be welcomed into various households and treated with drinks, this no longer obtains. Now, musicians stop outside the households, play for a while then move on to another. Diana also observed that the quality of the music has changed. There is more chanting and noise now as compared to times past when one would hear distinctly, a chorus of voices singing in response to the Chantwelle.

Mrs.Antoine believes that one of the reasons for the decline of the practice of the Sèwénal is that persons have become more self-centred. Many are no longer as welcoming of the performers as their forbearers. According to Mrs. Antoine people are now concerned about their new rug and furniture etc becoming soiled by the revelers.

Paul Elian believes that the tradition is still alive but under threat of demise. He attributes this to the fact that many of those who would be able to carry the tradition are too burdened by the responsibilities of employment away from the community to give the time to prepare. Since the downturn of the banana industry, many, including him, now work in Castries in the construction sector. Like French, Paul also laments the fact that the youth, although demonstrating an interest in the tradition do not commit to meeting early enough during the year to make the necessary preparations.

CONCLUSION

The cultural forms and practices of any territory are always in a state of constant change as a result of social, political and economic factors. The cultural practices discussed in this book are part of the evolution of communities and therefore affected by the modernization of those communities and the concomitant development and mobility of the people.

The Kèlè ritual is no longer practiced. The Papa Djab and Masquerade, although still performed for entertainment have lost their other function as a means by which the socially marginalized engaged the dominant discourse. The Koudmen, while still alive in many quarters is no longer a way of life throughout the island. Construction and farming are industries in which locals are entrepreneurs and the services of labour, linked now to the dictates of banks and mortgage companies, have become more specialized and professional. The Flower Societies have lost not only a significant number of their membership, but also their skill base; as the old practitioners become too old to participate and the youth venture into more modern preoccupations. Such has been the trend for many years with the cultural forms.

Yet, despite these changes, many of the forms persist and it is clear that Saint Lucians recognize the significance of those forms to the shape of their character and the projection of their identity. Thus the forms remain important to the island's cultural positioning and international profile. The award of the Nobel Prize in the year 1992 to Saint Lucian poet Derek Walcott provides a source of pride to Saint Lucian in the value and power of their culture.

Institutions such as the Folk Research Centre and the Cultural Development Foundation continue to play a major role in helping

Saint Lucians appreciate the importance of their culture to the development of national pride. Undoubtedly these institutions through their ability to attract state support as well the support of other donor agencies, have assisted in the sustenance of many of the cultural forms. The organization of workshops and festivals; as well as popular education activities helps keep the cultural forms and practices alive.

However, the 'interference' of the state sponsored institutions has also brought new dynamics into the organization of the cultural practices at the community level, subjecting the process of their development to the externally directed vagaries of politics and commerce. Many of the older folk who are carriers of the traditions have become suspicious that outsiders are merely interested in exploiting their heritage. They have come to recognize that their knowledge and skills are merely valued for their political and commercial capital. For this reason they are often reluctant to participate in community projects that are externally driven. This is hardly a surprising response from a people who have experienced a long history of exploitation by both the slave masters and subsequently by others who seek commercial and/or political power.

The recent thrust by Caribbean governments towards cultural tourism and the establishment of Creative Industries as a means of boosting foreign currency reserves and National Income have also brought renewed interest to the cultural forms. Conscious attempts are now being made to reproduce and pre-package traditional artistic forms into products that can be marketed to tourists and locals alike.

As the cultural forms and practices continue to respond to the new demands, we study them; examining as it were, our own reflections, how our images change in response to the new challenges. Irrespective of the adjustments to the costumes and the spaces; and the impact of the technology on our rhythms however, the cultural forms stir the Saint Lucian spirit. In so doing, they continually revive our memories of the strength of our ancestors who always adjusted remarkably, to the challenges of drastic change. Hopefully our policymakers will be mindful of this so that no matter what the changes; no matter what the new economic imperatives, we will safeguard the forms and practices through which we embody the spirits of revival and survival!

BIBLIOGRAPHY

Abrahams Roger D and John F. Szwed. *After Africa* New Haven and London: Yale University Press

Alleyne, Mervyn. *Roots of Jamaican Culture*. London: Pluto Press, 1988.

Alleyne, C. Mervyn. "The Role of Africa in the Construction of Identity in the

Caribbean" *Matatu-Journal for African Culture and Society*, Volume 27/28: A Pepperpot of Cultures. Aspects of Creolization in the Caribbean.

Anderson, Benedict. *Imagined Communities. London*: Verso, 1983

Anthony, Patrick. "The Flower Festivals of St. Lucia". *Folk Research Centre Culture and Society Series* Vol 1 Castries: 1990.

Ashcroft, Bill, Gareth Giffiths and Helen Tiffin. *The Empire Writes Back*. London and New York: Routledge, 1989

Avtar Brah, *Cartographies of Diaspora Contesting Identities,* London and New York: Routledge Taylor and Francis Group, 1996.

Baer, William *Conversations With Walcott*. Universty Press of Mississippi, 1996.

Bhabha, Homi. *The Location of Culture*. London and New York: Routledge, 1994

Baluntansky M. Kathleen and Marie Agnes Sourieau. *Caribbean Creolization: Reflections opn the Cultural Dynamics of language, Literature, and Identity* Gainesville: University of Florida Press and Jamaica: University of West Indies Press, 1998

Beckles, Hilary McD "Crop Over Fetes and Festivals in Caribbean Slavery", ed. Alvin O. Thompson *In The Shadow of the Plantation*. Kingston: Ian Randle, 2002

Bernabe, Jean with Confiant Raphael and Charmoiseau, Patrick. *In Praise of Creoleness*. (Baltimore: The Johns Hopkins University Press, 1990.

Brathwaite, Edward. *The Development of Creole Society in Jamaica 1770-1820*.Oxford: Clarendon Press, 1971.

Breen, Henry. St. Lucia Historical, Statistical and Descriptive. London: Frank Cass & Co. Ltd. 1970

Crahan, Margaret E. and Franklin W. Knight*Africa and the Caribbean The Legacies of a Link*.Baltimore: The John Hopkins University Press, 1999.

Dash, Michael J. "Anxious Insularity Identity Politics and Creolization in the Caribbean" *Matatu Journal for African Culture and Society*, Vol 27-8 A pepperpot of Cultures Aspects of Creolization in the Caribbean.

Certeau de, Michel. *The Practice of Everyday Life*, University of Califonia Press, 2002, 94.

Foucault, Michel. *The Foucault Reader*. New York: Pantheon Books, 1984.

Frantz, Fanon *Black Skin, White Masks*. London: Pluto Press, 1952.

Franz Fanon, *The Wretched of The Earth*.Great Britain: Presence Africaine, 1963.

Gallagher, Mary *Place and Displacement in Caribbean Writing in French* New York: Rodopi, 200

Gilbert, Helen. *Postcolonial Plays.* New York: Routledge, 2001.

Gilbert, Helen and Tompkins, Joanne *Post Colonial Drama theory, practice, politics.* London: Routledge, 1996

Gilroy, Paul. *Between Camps Nations, Cultures and the Allure of Race.* London: Routledge, 2000

Gilroy, Paul. *The Black Atlantic.* London and New York: Verso, 1993

Glissant,Edward (Interview with Label France. *http://www.diplomatie. gouv.fr/en/france_159/label-france_2554/label-france-issues_2555/ label-france-no.-38_4204/feature-together-into-the-21st-century_4285/exchanging_4286/the-cultural-creolization-of-the-world.-interview-with-edouard-glissant_6589.html*

Gramsci, Antonio. Selections from Cultural Writings. Cambridge, Massachusettes: Havard University Press. 1991.

Gramsci, Antonio. The Antonio Gramsci Reader. David Forgacs. NY: New York University Press, 2000.

Gray, Ann. *Research Practice for Cultural Studies* London: SAGE Publications, 2003.

Geertz, Clifford, The Interpretation of Cultures.

Grossberg, Lawerence. Nelson Cary and Paula Treichler. *Cultural Studies* New York: Routledge, 1992.

Hall, Stuart. *Representation: Cultural Representations and Signifying Practices, London: SAGE Puiblications,* 1997

Hall, Stuart. "Thinking the Diaspora : Home Thoughts from Abroad". Small Axe No.6 Sept 1999

Hammer, Robert D. *Perspectives On Derek Walcott* (Washington: Three Continents Press, 1993.

Harris, Wilson "Creoleness the Crossroads of a Civilization?" ed. Baluntansky M. Kathleen and Marie Agnes Sourieau. *Caribbean Creolization: Reflections opn the Cultural Dynamics of language, Literature, and Identity.* Gainesville: University of Florida Press and Jamaica: University of West Indies Press, 1998

Hurley, Anthony E, *Through A Black Veil—Readings In French Caribbean Poetry.* Trenton NJ: Africa World Press, INC 2000

Irele, Abiola. *Aime Cesaire Cahier D'un Retour Au Pays Natal.* Ibadan: new Horn Press Ltd, 1994.

Jolivert, Marie Jose. "Creolization and Intercultural Dynamics in French Guiana" ed. Sahlini Puri, *Marginal Migrations.* Oxford: Macmillan Publishers, 2003

King, Bruce *Derek Walcott A Caribbean Life.* New York: Oxford University Press Inc, 2000

Johnson, Howard. After The Crossing. Immigrants and Minorities in Caribbean Creole Society. London: Howard Cass 7Co. Ltd., 1988.

Lalla, Barbara. "Creole Representation in Literary Discourse" ed. Robertson Ian and Hazel Simmons-McDonald. *Exploring the Boundaries of Caribban Creole Languages,* Kingston:University of the West Indies Press, 2006

Lewis-Warner, Maureen. *Guinea'a Other Suns.* Dover: The Majority Press, 1991.

Massey, Doreen. *Space, Place and Gender.* Minneapolis: University of Minnesota Press, 1994

McDonald-Simmons, Hazel "Cultural Preservation and Language Reclamation: The St. Lucian Paradox" conference "Rethinking Caribbean Culture" UWI, Cave Hill June 4-8, 2001.

Mauvois, Georges *Man Chomil.* Schoelcher: Presses Universaires Creoles, 1992

Meeks, B and F. Lindhall. *New Caribbean Thought.* Kingston: UWI Press, 2001

Mintz W. Sidney and Richard Price. *The Birth of African American Culture.* Boston: Beacon Press, 1976

Morley, David and kuan-Hsing Chen Hall, Stuart. *Critical Dialogues in Cultural Studies.* London: Routledge, 1996.

Olmos Fernandez Margeurite & Gebert-Paravisini Lizabeth, *Creole Religions of the Caribbean An Introduction from Vodou and Santeria to Obeah and Espiritismo.* New York: New York University Press, 2003

Padmini, Mongia. *Contemporary Postcolonial Theory.* London: Arnold, 1996.

Pereira, Joseph. "Introducing Cultural Studies at UWI: Reflections on an Experience" "Rethinking Caribbean Culture" UWI, Cave Hill June 4-8, 2001.

Puri, Shalini. *The Caribbean Postcolonial. New York:* PALGRAVE MACMILLAN, 2004.

Said, Edward. *Culture and Imperialism.* New York: Vintage Books, 1993.

Sarnecki, Judith Holland. "Mastering the Masters: Aimé Césaire's Creolization of Shakespeare's *The Tempest.*" *French Review* 74, no. 2 December 2000

Saukko, Paula. *Doing Research in Cultural Studies. London:* SAGE Publications, 2003.

Sheperd, Verene S and Glen L. Richards. *Questioning Creole Creolisation Discourses in Caribbean Culture.* Kingston: Ian Randle Publishers, 2002

Smith-Tuhiwai, Linda. *Decolonizing Methodologies.* London: Zed Books, 1999.

Strong, Laura. "Egungun: The Masked Ancestors of the Yoruba." *http://www.mythicarts.com/writing/Egungun.htm*

Stone S.J. Judy *Theatre.* London: The Macmillan Press LTD, 1994

Taylor, Patrick. *Nation Dance Religion, Identity and Cultural Difference in the Caribbean.* Indianapolis: Indiana University Press, 2001

Terada, Rei. *Derek Walcott's Poetry American Mimicry.* Boston: Northwestern University Press, 1992

The Literary Encyclopedia www.litencyc.com/php/sworks. php?rec=true&UID=3088-17k

The Alan Lomax Collection

The Nobel Prize Internet Archive

Walcott, Derek. *What The Twilight Says.* London: Faber and Faber, 1998

Walcott, Derek. *Dream on Monkey Mountain and Other Plays.* New York: Farrar, Straus and Giroux, 1970

Ward, Graham. *The Certeau Reader.* Massachusettes: Blackwell Publishers, 2000

Werbner, Pnina and Tariq Modood *Debating Cultural Hybridity.* London and New Jersey: Zen Books, 1997

Wing, Betsy *Black Salt*. USA: The University of Michagan Press, 1983

(http://www.guardian.co.uk/society/2007/sep/23
http://en.wikipedia.org/wiki/Shango http://en.wikipedia.org/wiki/
Ogoun

Endnotes

1. Brathwaite, Edward Kamau. *Folk Culture of the Slaves of Jamaica* (New Beacon Books London Poet of Spain 1974 17

2. Mintz W. Sidney and Richard Price *The Birth of African American Culture*. Boston: Beacon Press, 1976 23

3. Ibid 23

4. Gilroy, Paul. *Between Camps, Nations, Cultures and the Allure of Race* London: Routledge, 2000 99

5. Walcott, Derek, "The Flight of Pelicans" address delivered at the Rat Island Foundation Frund Raising Banquet at the Great House on August 26, 1993. Folk Research Centre Bulletin Volume 3 Number 2 July-December 1993) p74

6. Mintz W. Sidney and Richard Price *The Birth of African American Culture*. Boston: Beacon Press, 1976 57-58

7. Harold Simmons, St. Lucian folklorist collaborated with American folklorist, Alan Lomax to record many folk songs and stories on the island. The data was later compiled into a collection of CDs, copies of which were donated to the Folk Research Centre in St. Lucia. See website (http://www.loc.gov/folklife/lomax/) for information on the complete Alan Lomax Collection where this recording can be accessed.

8. Melville J. Herskovits, *The Myth of the Negro Past* Boston: Beacon Press, 1941) 63

9. See website (http://www.loc.gov/folklife/lomax/) for more information on the complete Alan Lomax Collection.

10. Gilroy, Paul. *Between Camps, Nations, Cultures and the Allure of Race* London: Routledge, 2000 191

11. See website (http://www.loc.gov/folklife/lomax/) for information on the complete Alan Lomax Collection where this recording can be accessed.

12. ibid

13. Kremser, Manfred *RESEARCH IN ETHNOGRATHY AND ETHNOHISTORY OF ST.LUCIA* ed. Manfred Kremser &Karl R. WERNHART (Verlag Ferdinand Berger & Sohne Horn-Wein 1986 78

14. Simmons, Harold F. C. 42

15. Ibid 44

16. Kremser, Manfred *RESEARCH IN ETHNOGRATHY AND ETHNOHISTORY OF ST.LUCIA* edited by Manfred Kremser &Karl R. WERNHART (Verlag Ferdinand Berger & Sohne Horn-Wein 1986 83

17. Ibid 83
18. Lewis-Warner Maureen Guinea's Other Suns. Dover : The Majority Press, 1991. 32
19. Ibid 32
20. Ibid 32
21. Bettelheim, Judith. " Jamaica Jonkonnu and Related Caribbean Festivals." *Africa and the Caribbean The Legacies of a Link.* Ed Margaret E. Crahan and Franklin W. Knight. Baltimore: The John Hopkins University Press, 1999. 80
22. Ibid 81
23. Ibid 96
24. Ibid 83
25. "Columbus Square" now renamed "Derek Walcott Square" is a park in the Centre of Castries the capital city of St. Lucia.
26. The Chac Chac is a cylindrical container of beads that is uses as a percussive instrument. In some countries it is called the maracas.
27. The Ti Bwa(Bois) is an instrument made up of a dry a piece of dry bamboo upon which the musician strikes two sticks to a steady rhythm.
28. 31 Olmos Fernandez Margeurite & Gebert-Paravisini Lizabeth, *Creole Religions of the Caribbean An Introduction from Vodou and Santeria to Obeah and Espiritismo.* New York: New York University Press, 2003
29. Anthony, Anthony, Patrick. "The Flower Festivals of St. Lucia". *Folk Research Centre Culture and Society Series* Vol 1 Castries: 1990. 14-21
30. Olmos Fernandez Margeurite & Gebert-Paravisini Lizabeth, *Creole Religions of the Caribbean An Introduction from Vodou and Santeria to Obeah and Espiritismo.* New York: New York University Press, 2003 27
31. Ibid 27
32. Ibid 27
33. Ibid 27
34. Gilroy, Paul. *Between Camps, Nations, Cultures and the Allure of Race* London: Routledge, 2000 99
35. Anthony, Patrick. "The Flower Festivals of St. Lucia". *Folk Research Centre Culture and Society Series* Vol 1 Castries: 1990. 2
36. Ibid 2
37. Abrahams Roger D and John F. Szwed. *After Africa* New Haven: Yale University Press 230
38. Ibid 230 Ibid Bettelheim, Judith. "Jamaican Jonkonnu and Related Caribbean Festivals". *Africa and the Caribbean The Legacies of a Link.*

Ed. Margaret E. Crahan and Franklin W. Knight.Baltimore: The John Hopkins University Press, 1999.

39. Breen, H. Henry. *St. Lucia, Historical, Statistical, and Descriptive. After Africa* Ed. Roger D. Abrahams and John F. Szwed. New Haven: Yale University Press . . . 263

40. Ibid 263

41. Ibid 264

42. Massey, Doreen. *Space, Place and Gender.* Minneapolis: University of Minnesota Press, 1994. 264

43. Hall, Stuart. " What is this 'black' in black popular culture?" Stuart Hall Critical Dialogues in Cultural Studies. Ed. David Morley and Kuan-Hsing Chen. London: Routledge, 1996. 468

44. Simmons Harold, *Selected Writings of Harold F. C. Simmons* compiled by Didacus Jules unpublished (Folk Research Centre) 35

45. Ibid 36

46. Ibid 36